POLLY HON

A DRAMATI

O F O N E A C T.

As it is ACTED at the

T H E A T R E-R O Y A L

I N

D R U R Y - L A N E.

The T H I R D E D I T I O N.

With A L T E R A T I O N S.

L O N D O N :

Printed for T. BECKET, and P. A. DEHONDT, in the
Strand. M D CC LXII.

Printing Statement:

Due to the very old age and scarcity of this book,
many of the pages may be hard to read due to the
blurring of the original text, possible missing pages,
missing text, dark backgrounds and other issues
beyond our control.

Because this is such an important and rare work, we
believe it is best to reproduce this book regardless of
its original condition.

Thank you for your understanding.

PREFACE.

AFTER expreſſing my Gratitude to the Publick for the kind reception they have given
to Miſs Honeycombe, and returning thanks to the
Performers for their care and uncommon excellence
in the Repreſentation, I did not think of adding
any thing further by way of Preface ; but my
Publiſher inſiſts on the neceſſity of my ſaying ſome-
thing in behalf of the Piece, which, I think, ought
to ſpeak for itſelf, and that my friend's ſcheme is
much of the ſame colour with Bayes's practice of
printing papers *to inſinuate the Plot into the Boxes.*
It has been uſual with the Writers of the French
Theatre, it is true, to tack Examens of their
Plays, like a ſting or *melius non tangere* to the Criticks, to the tail of them. But why need an Engliſh Author put himſelf to that trouble, when the
learned and impartial gentlemen of the Reviews
are ſo ready to take it off his hands, unleſs it were,
like Dryden, to turn the thunder of the Critick's
own artillery againſt himſelf, and to confute or
anticipate his cenſures, by proving the Fable, Characters, Sentiments, and Language, to be excellent, or, if indeed there were ſome parts of it in-
ferior to the reſt, ſuch parts were purpoſely *under-
written,* in order to ſet off the ſuperior to more
advantage ? This, indeed, Dryden has often done,
and done ſo inimitably, that I ſhall not attempt
it

it after him. To the Gentlemen, therefore, above-mentioned, the self-impannelled Jury of the English Court of Criticism, without Challenge, I put myself on my Trial for the High Crime of writing for the Stage, trusting that their candour will send me a good deliverance.

I could, indeed, in compliance with the request of my Publisher, have obliged the Publick, by printing, entire, an original Manuscript, now in my possession, containing several strictures on the following scenes ; being no other than a Letter from my Mother, occasioned by the first night's representation, which, like most other first nights, was nothing more than a Publick Rehearsal, with ten thousand fears and apprehensions that never attend a private one. That Good Gentlewoman, hurt at the confusion, and in pain for my success, tells me with much warmth, and as dogmatically as any Male Critick could possibly do, that She is astonished at my attempting to violate the received laws of the Drama——That the *Catastrophe* (that was really her word) is directly contrary to all known rules—That the several Characters, instead of being dismissed, one by one, should have been industriously kept together, to make a bow to the audience at the dropping of the curtain——That, notwithstanding any confusion, created by the Girl's whimsical passion for Novels, in the course of the Piece, all parties should be perfectly reconciled to each other at last. Polly, having manifested her affection for him, should, to be sure, have been married to Scribble ; and the Parents should have been thoroughly, though suddenly, appeased by the declared reformation of both. Ledger might, with much propriety and great probability, have been disposed of to the Nurse : and the whole Piece,

Piece, inftead of concluding bluntly with a fen-
tence in Profe, fhould have been tagged with a
Couplet or Two; and then every thing would
have gone off fmoothly and roundly, *à la mode
du Théatre.*

Having thus prefented the Publick with a fmall
fpecimen of my good Mother's talents for Criti-
cifm, I fhall not, by attempting to anfwer them,
heap Remarks upon Remarks;. rather chufing to
leave Her and all other Criticks, Male and Female, to meditate on the following extract from
Ben Johnfon; but muft, at the fame time, defire
not to be underftood to take to myfelf that confi-
dence, with which he prefumes to fpeak of his own
abilities.

  " Though my Cataftrophe may, in the ftrict
" rigour of Comick Law, meet with cenfure; I
" defire the learned and charitable Critick, to have
" fo much faith in me, to think it was done of
" induftry: for, with what eafe I could have va-
" ried it nearer his fcale (but that I fear to boaft
" my own faculty) I could here infert."

To this quotation I fhall add a fhort ftory, and
then conclude my Preface with an Extract from
the Catalogue of one of our moft popular Circulating Libraries; from which Extract the reader
may, without any great degree of fhrewdnefs, ftrain
the moral of this performance. The ftory is as
follows.   -

A Nobleman of Madrid, being prefent at the
Spanifh Comedy, fell afleep during the firft act,
and never woke again till the end of the play.
Then rubbing his eyes, and obferving his friends
laughing at the hearty nap he had taken, he cried
out, *How now? Gentlemen! What! Is it* OVER
then? Are the Actors all MARRIED?.

E X T R A C T.

EXTRACT.

A Ccomplifh'd Rake, or the modern fine Gentleman.

Adventures of Mifs Polly B—ch—rd and Samuel Tyrrel, efq.

Adventures of Jerry Buck.

Adventures of Dick Hazard.

Adventures of Jack Smart.

Adventures of Lindamira, a Lady of Quality.

Adventures of David Simple.

Adventures of a Turk.

Adventures of Daphnis and Chloe.

Advenures of Prince Cleremont and Mad. de Ravezan.

Adventures of Mr. Loveil.

Adventures of Jofeph Andrews.

Adventures of Hamilton Murray.

Adventures of a Rake.

Adventures of a Cat.

Adventures of a Black Coat.

Adventures of Frank Hammond.

Adventures of Mr. George Edwards, a Creole.

Adventures of a Valet.

Adventures of Capt. Greenland.

Adventures of Roderick Random.

Adventures of Peregrine Pickle.

Adventures of Ferdinand Count Fathom.

Agenor and Ifmeaa, or the War of the tender paffions.

Amelia, by Mr. Fielding.

Amelia, or the diftreffed Wife.

Amours of Philander and Sylvia, or Love-letters between a Nobleman and his Sifter.

Amorous Friars, or the Intrigues of a Convent.

Anti-Gallican, or the Hiftory and Adventures of Harry Cobham.

Anti-Pamela, or feigned Innocence detected.

Apparition, or Female Cavalier. a Story founded on Facts.

Auction.

Beauty put to its Shifts, or the Young Virgin's Rambles, being feveral Years Adventures of Mifs * * * * in England and Portugal.

Bracelet, or the Fortunate Difcovery ; being the Hiftory of Mifs Polly * * *.

Brothers.

Bubbled Knights, or fuccefsful Contrivances ; plainly evincing, in two familiar inftances lately tranfacted in this Metropolis, *the Folly and Unreafonablenefs of Parents laying a Reftraint upon their Childrens Inclinations in the affairs of Love and Marriage.*

Card.

Chiron, or the mental Optician.

Chit-chat, or a feries of interefting Adventures.

Chryfal, or the Adventures of a Guinea, with curious Anecdotes.

Clariffa, or the Hiftory of a young Lady ; comprehending the moft important Concerns

History

History and Adventures of Frank Hammond.
History of Jasper Banks.
History of J. Trueman, Esq; and Miss Peggy Williams.
History of Sir Harry Herald and Sir Edw. Haunch.
History of Will Ramble, a Libertine.
History of Miss Polly Willis,
History of my own Life.
History of Lucy Wellers.
History of a Fair Greek, who was taken out of a Seraglio at Constantinople.
History of Hai Ebor Yokdhan, an Indian Prince.
History of the human Heart, or Adventures of a young Gentleman.
History of Charlote Summers.
History of Cornelia.
History of Tom Jones a Foundling.
History of Tom Jones in his married State.
History of two modern Adventurers.
History of Sir Roger, and his Son Joe.
History of Miss Sally Sable.
History of Mira, Daughter of Marcio.
History of Amanda, by a young Lady.
History of a Woman of Quality, or the Adventures of Lady Frail.
History of Pompey the Little, or the Adventures of a Lap-Dog.
History of Wilhelmina Susannah Dormer.
History of Porcia.
History of the Countess of Dellwyn.

History of Ophelia.
History of the Marchioness de Pompadour, Mistress to the French King, and first Lady of Honour to the Queen.
History of Tom Fool.
History of the *Intrigues* and *Gallantries* of Christiana, Queen of Sweden.
History of Jack Connor.
History of Miss Betsy Thoughtless.
Histories of some of the Penitents in the Magdalen-House.
Jilts, or Female Fortune-hunters.
Impetuous Lover, or the Guiltless Parracide; shewing *to what Lengths Love may run*, and the extreme Folly of forming schemes for Futurity.
Intriguing Coxcomb.
Journey through every Stage of Life.
Juvenile Adventures of David Ranger, Esq.
Juvenile Adventures of Miss Kitty Fisher.
Lady's Advocate, or Wit and Beauty a Match for Treachery and Inconstancy; containing a Series of Gallantries, Intrigues, and Amours, fortunate and sinister; Quarrels and Reconciliations between Lovers; conjugal Plagues and Comforts, Vexations and Endearments; with many remarkable Incidents and Adventures, the Effects of Love and Jealousy, Fidelity and Inconstancy.
Ladies Tales.
Life and Adventures of Miranda.

Life's.

P R O L O G U E.

Spoken by Mr. K I N G

HITHER, in days of yore, from Spain or France
Came a dread Sorceress; her name, ROMANCE:
O'er Britain's Isle her wayward spells She cast,
And Common Sense in magick chain bound fast.
In mad Sublime did each fond Lover wooe,
And in Heroicks ran each Billet-Doux:
High deeds of Chivalry their sole Delight,
Each Fair a Maid Distrest, each Swain a Knight:
Then might Statira Orondates see,
At Tilts and Tournaments, arm'd Cap-a-pe.,
She too, on Milk-white Palfrey, Lance in hand,
A Dwarf to guard her, pranc'd about the land.

This Fiend to quell, his sword Cervantes drew;
A trusty Spanish Blade, Toledo true:
Her Talismans and Magick Wand He broke—
Knights, Genii, Castles——vanished into smoke.

But

PROLOGUE:

But now, the dear delight of later years,
The younger sister of ROMANCE appears:
Less solemn is her air, her drift the same,
And NOVEL her enchanting, charming, Name.
ROMANCE might strike our grave Forefathers pomp,
But NOVEL for our Buck and lively-Romp!
Cassandra's Folios now no longer read,
See, Two neat Pocket Volumes in their stead!
And then so sentimental is the Stile,
So chaste, yet so bewitching all the while!
Plot, and elopement, passion, rape, and rapture,
The total sum of ev'ry dear—dear—Chapter.
'Tis not alone the Small-Talk and the Smart,
'Tis NOVEL most beguiles the Female Heart.
Miss reads—she melts—she sighs—Love steals upon her—
And then—Alas, poor Girl!—good night, poor Honour!

   " * Thus of our Polly having lightly spoke,
" Now for our Author!—but without a joke.
" Though Wits and Journals, who ne'er fibb'd before,
" Have laid this Bantling at a certain door,
" Where, lying store of faults, they'd fain heap more,
" I now declare it, as a serious truth,
" 'Tis the first folly of a simple Youth,
" Caught and deluded by our harlot plays:—
" Then crush not in the shell this infant Bayes!
" Exert your favour to a young Beginner,
" Nor use the Stripling like a Batter'd Sinner!

* These Lines were added by Mr. GARRICK, on its being
reported, that he was the Author of this Piece: and, however
humorous and poetical, contain as strict matter of fact as the
dullest Prose.

PERSONS.

HONEYCOMBE,	Mr. YATES.
LEDGER,	Mr. BRANSBY.
SCRIBBLE,	Mr. KING.

Mrs. HONEYCOMBE,	Mrs. KENNEDY.
POLLY,	Miss POPE.
NURSE,	Mrs. BRADSHAW.

POLLY HONEYCOMBE,

A Dramatick NOVEL of One ACT.

****

SCENE I.

An Apartment in HONEYCOMBE's *House.*

POLLY, *with a Book in her Hand.*

WELL faid, Sir George!—O the dear
man!—But fo——" With thefe words
" the enraptur'd baronet [*reading*] con-
" cluded his declaration of love."—So!
—" But what heart can imagine,
" [*reading*] what tongue defcribe, or what pen de-
" lineate, the amiable confufion of Emilia?"—
Well! now for it!——" Reader, if thou art a
" courtly reader, thou haft feen, at polite tables,
iced

" iced cream crimfoned with rafberries; or, if thou
" art an uncourtly reader; thou haft feen the rofy-
" finger'd morning dawning in the golden eaft;"
—Dawning in the golden eaft!—Very pretty;—
" Thou haft feen, perhaps, [*reading*] the artificial
" vermilion on the cheeks of Cleora, or the ver-
" milion of nature on thofe of Sylvia; thou haft
" feen—in a word, the lovely face of Emilia was
" overfpread with blufhes."———This is a moft
beautiful paffage, I proteft! Well, a Novel for
my money! Lord, lord, my ftupid Papa has no
tafte. He has no notion of humour, and character, and the fenfibility of delicate feeling. [*affec-
tedly*] And then Mama,—but where was I?—Oh
here—" Overfpread with blufhes. [*reading*] Sir
" George, touched at her confufion, gently feized
" her hand, and foftly preffing it to his bofom,
" [*acting it as fhe reads*] where the pulfes of his
" heart beat quick, throbbing with tumultuous
" paffion, in a plaintive tone of voice breathed out,
" Will you not anfwer me, Emilia?"———Tender
creature!———" She, half raifing [*reading and acting*] her downcaft eyes, and half inclining her
" averted head, faid in faltering accents—Yes,
" Sir!"—Well, now!—" Then gradually recover-
" ing, with ineffable fweetnefs fhe prepared to ad-
" drefs him; when Mrs. Jenkinfon bounced into
" the room, threw down a fet of china in her hur-
" ry, and ftrewed the floor with porcelain frag-
" ments: then turning Emilia round and round,
" whirled her out of the apartment in an inftant,
" and ftruck Sir George dumb with aftonifhment
" at her appearance. She raved; but the baronet
" refuming his accuftomed effrontery———

Enter

Enter NURSE.

Oh, Nurfe! I am glad to fee you!—Well, and
how——

NURSE.

Well, Chicken!

POLLY.

Tell me, tell me all this inftant. Did you fee
him? Did you give him my letter? Did he
write? Will he come? Shall I fee him? Have
you got the anfwer in your pocket? Have you—

NURSE.

Bleffings on her, how her tongue runs!

POLLY.

Nay, but come, dear Nurfee, tell me, what did
he fay?

NURSE.

Say? why he took the letter——

POLLY.

Well!

NURSE.

And kifs'd it a thoufand times, and read it a
thoufand times, and——

POLLY.

Oh charming!

NURSE.

And ran about the room, and bleft himfelf,
and, heaven preferve us, curft himfelf, and——

POLLY.

Very fine! very fine!

NURSE.

And vowed he was the moft miferable creature

B   upon

upon earth, and the happieſt man in the world, and——

P O L L Y.

Prodigiouſly fine! excellent! My dear, dear Nurſee! [*Kiſſing her.*] Come, give me the letter.

N U R S E.

Letter, Chicken! what letter?

P O L L Y.

The anſwer to mine. Come then! [*Impatiently.*]

N U R S E.

I have no letter. He had ſuch a *peramble* to write, by my troth I could not ſtay for it.

P O L L Y.

Pſhah!

N U R S E.

How ſoon you're affronted now! he ſaid he'd ſend it ſome time to-day.

P O L L Y.

Send it ſome time to-day!—I wonder now, [*as if muſing.*] how he will convey it. Will he ſqueeze it, as he did the laſt, into the chicken-houſe in the garden? Or will he write it in lemon-juice, and ſend it in a book, like blank paper? Or will he throw it into the houſe, incloſed in an orange? Or will he——

N U R S E.

Heavens bleſs her, what a ſharp wit ſhe has!

P O L L Y.

I have not read ſo many books for nothing. Novels, Nurſee, Novels! A Novel is the only thing to teach a girl life, and the way of the world, and elegant fancies, and love to the end of the chapter.

N U R S E.

N U R S E.

Yes, yes, you are always reading your simple story-books. The *Ventures* of Jack this, and the history of Betfy t'other, and fir Humphrys, and women with hard christian names. You had better read your prayer-book, Chicken.

P O L L Y,

Why so I do; but I'm reading this now—[*Looking into the book.*] " She raved, but the baronet"—I really think I love Mr. Scribble as well as Emilia did Sir George.—Do you think, Nurfee, I should have had such a good notion of love so early, if I had not read Novels?—Did not I make a conquest of Mr. Scribble in a single night at a dancing ? But my crofs Papa will hardly ever let me go out. —And then, I know life as well as if I had been in the Beau Monde all my days. I can tell the nature of a masquerade as well as if I had been at twenty. I long for a mobbing scheme with Mr. Scribble in the two-shilling gallery, or a snug party a little way out of town in a post-chaife———and then, I have such a head full of intrigues and contrivances! Oh, Nurfee, a Novel is the only thing.

N U R S E.

Contrivances! ay, marry, you have need of contrivances. Here are your Papa and Mama fully refolved to marry you to young Mr. Ledger, Mr. Simeon the rich Jew's wife's nephew, and all the while your head runs upon nothing but Mr. Scribble.

P O L L Y.

A fiddle stick's end for Mr. Ledger ! I tell you what, Nurfee, I'll marry Mr. Scribble, and not

marry

marry Mr. Ledger, whether Papa and Mama chuſe it or no.—And how do you think I'll contrive it?

NURSE.

How? Chicken!

POLLY.

Why, don't you know?

NURSE.

No, indeed.

POLLY.

And can't you gueſs?

NURSE.

No, by my troth, not I.

POLLY.

O lord, 'tis the commoneſt thing in the world. —I intend to elope.

NURSE.

Elope! Chicken, what's that?

POLLY.

Why, in the vulgar phraſe, run away,——— that's all.

NURSE.

Mercy on us!——Run away!

POLLY.

Yes, run away, to be ſure. Why there's nothing in that, you know. Every girl elopes when her parents are obſtinate and ill-natur'd about marrying her. It was juſt ſo with Betſy Thompſon, and Sally Wilkins, and Clarinda, and Leonora in the hiſtory of Dick Careleſs, and Julia in the Adventures of Tom Ramble, and fifty others—Did not they all elope? and ſo will I too. I have as much right to elope as they had, for I have as much love, and as much ſpirit, as the beſt of them.

NURSE.

NURSE.

Why, Mr. Scribble's a fine man to be sure, a gentleman every inch of him!

POLLY.

So he is, a dear charming man!—Will you elope too, Nurfee?

NURSE.

Not for the varfal world. Suppofe now, Chicken, your Papa and Mama——

POLLY.

What care I for Papa and Mama? Have not they been married and happy long enough ago? and are they not ftill coaxing, and fondling, and kiffing each other all the day long?—Where's my dear Love, [*mimicking*.] My Beauty? fays Papa, hobbling along with his crutch-headed cane, and his old gouty legs: Ah, my fweeting, my precious Mr. Honeycombe, d'ye love your nown dear wife? fays Mama; and then they fqueeze their hard-hands to each other, and their old eyes twinkle, and they're as loving as Darby and Joan, —efpecially if Mama has had a cordial or two—— Eh! Nurfee!

NURSE.

Oh fie, Chicken!

POLLY.

And then perhaps, in comes my utter averfion, Mr. Ledger, with his news from the Change, and his Change-alley wit, and his thirty *per cent.* [*mimicking*.] and ftocks have rifen one and a half and three-eighths.—I'll tell you what, Nurfee! they would make fine charaƈters for a Novel, all three of them.

NURSE.

N U R S E.

Ah, you're a gracelefs bird!—But I muft go down ftairs, and watch if the coaft's clear, in cafe of a letter.

P O L L Y.

Could not you go to Mr. Scribble's again after it?

N U R S E.

Again! indeed, Mrs. Hot-upon't!

P O L L Y.

Do now, my dear Nurfee, pray do! and call at the Circulating Library as you go along, for the reft of this Novel—The Hiftory of Sir George Truman and Emilia—and tell the bookfeller to be fure to fend me the Britifh Amazon, and Tom Faddle, and the reft of the new Novels this-winter, as foon as ever they come out.

N U R S E.

Ah, pife on your naughty Novels! I fay. [*Exit,*

P O L L Y.

Ay, go now, my dear Nurfee, go, there's a good woman.—What an old fool it is! with her pife on it—and fie, Chicken—and no, by my troth—[*mimicking.*]——Lord! what a ftrange houfe I live in! not a foul in it, except myfelf, but what are all queer animals, quite droll creatures. There's Papa and Mama, and the old foolifh Nurfe.—— [*Re-enter* Nurse *with a band-box.*] Oh, Nurfee, what brings you back fo foon? What have you got there?

N U R S E.

Mrs. Commode's 'prentice is below, and has brought home your new cap and ruffles, Chicken!

P O L L Y.

POLLY.

Let me fee—let me fee—[*opening the box.*] Well,
I fwear this is a mighty pretty cap, a fweet pair of
flying lappets! Aren't they, Nurfee?——Ha!
what's this? [*locking into the box.*]—Oh charming!
a letter! did not I tell you fo?——Let's fee—let's
fee——(*opening the letter haftily—it contains three or
four fheets.*) " Joy of my foul——only hope——
" eternal blifs—[*dipping into different places.*] The
" cruel blafts of coynefs and difdain blow out the
" flame of love, but then the virgin breath of
" kindnefs and compaffion blows it in again."—
Prodigious pretty! isn't it, Nurfee? [*turning over
the leaves.*]

NURSE.

Yes, that is pretty,—but what a deal there is
on't! It's an old faying and a true one, the more
there's faid the lefs there's done. Ah, they wrote
otherguefs fort of letters, when I was a girl!
[*while fhe talks Polly reads.*]

POLLY.

Lord, Nurfee, if it was not for Novels and Love-
letters, a girl would have no ufe for her writing and
reading.—But what's here? [*reading.*] Poetry !—
" *Well may I cry out with Alonzo in the Revenge—*
" *Where didft thou fteel thofe eyes? From heaven?*
" *Thou didft, and 'tis religion to adore them!*"
Excellent! oh! he's a dear Man.

NURSE.

Ay, to be fure!—But you forget your letter-
carrier below; fhe'll never bring you another, if
you don't fpeak to her kindly.

POLLY.

Speak to her! why, I'll give her fix-pence, woman! Tell her I am coming.—I will but juft read
my letter over five or fix times, and go to her.—Oh,
he's

he's a charming man ! [*reading.*] Very fine ! very pretty !—He writes as well as Bob Lovelace !—[*kiffing the letter.*] Oh, dear, fweet Mr. Scribble !

[*Exit.*

Scene changes to another Apartment.

HONEYCOMBE *and Mrs.* HONEYCOMBE *at breakfaft—*HONEYCOMBE *reading the News-paper.*

Mrs. HONEYCOMBE.

My dear ! [*peevifhly.*]

HONEYCOMBE.

What d'ye fay, my Love ? [*ftill reading.*]

Mrs. HONEYCOMBE.

You take no Notice of me.—Lay by that filly paper—put it down—come then—drink your tea:—You don't love me now.

HONEYCOMBE.

Ah ! my beauty ! [*looking very fondly.*]

Mrs. HONEYCOMBE.

Do you love your own dear wife ? [*tenderly.*]

HONEYCOMBE.

Dearly.——She knows I do.——Don't you, my beauty ?

Mrs. HONEYCOMBE.

Ah, you're a dear, dear man ! [*rifing and kiffing him.*] He does love her—and he's her own hufband—and fhe loves him moft dearly and tenderly——that fhe does. [*kiffing him.*]

HONEYCOMBE.

My beauty ! I have a Piece of news for you.

Mrs. HONEY-

Mrs. HONEYCOMBE.

What is it, my Sweeting?

HONEYCOMBE.

The Paper here fays, that young Tom Seaton, of Alderfgate-Street, was married yefterday at Bow-Church, to Mifs Fairly of Cornhill.

Mrs. HONEYCOMBE.

A flaunting, flaring huffy! fhe a hufband!——

HONEYCOMBE.

But what does my Beauty think of her own Daughter?

Mrs. HONEYCOMBE.

Of our Polly? Sweeting!

HONEYCOMBE.

Ay, Polly: What fort of a wife d'ye think fhe'll make? my Love!—I concluded every thing with Mr. Simeon yefterday, and expect Mr. Ledger every minute.

Mrs. HONEYCOMBE.

Think, my Sweetings!—why, I think, if fhe loves him half fo well as I do my own dear man, that fhe'll never fuffer him out of her fight—that fhe'll look at him with pleafure—[*they both ogle fondly.*]—and love him—and kifs him—and fondle him—oh, my dear, it's impoffible to fay how dearly I love you. [*kiffing and fondling him.*]

Enter LEDGER.

LEDGER.

Heyday! what now, good folks, what now? Are you fo much in Arrear? or are you paying off principal and intereft both at once?

C   HONEY.

HONEYCOMBE.

My dear!——Confider——Mr. Ledger is——

Mrs. HONEYCOMBE.

What fignifies Mr. Ledger?—He is one of the family, you know, my Sweeting!

LEDGER.

Ay, fo I am,—never mind me—never mind me.—Tho', by the bye, I fhould be glad of fomebody to make much of me too. Where's Mifs Polly?

HONEYCOMBE.

That's right—that's right.——Here, John!

Enter JOHN.

Where's Polly?

JOHN.

In her own room, Sir.

HONEYCOMBE.

Tell her to come here——and hark ye, John! while Mr. Ledger ftays, I am not at home to any body elfe. [*Exit* JOHN.

LEDGER.

Not at home!—are thofe your ways?—If I was to give fuch a Meffage to my fervant, I fhould ex-pect a commiffion of bankruptcy out against me the next day.

HONEYCOMBE.

Ay, you men of large dealings—it was fo with me, when I was in bufinefs.——But where's this girl? what can fhe be about?——My Beauty, do ftep yourfelf, and fend her here immediately.

Mrs. HONEYCOMBE.

I will, my Sweeting! [*offering to kifs him.*]

HONEY.

HONEYCOMBE.

Nay, my Love, not now——

Mrs. HONEYCOMBE.

Why not now ?—I will. [*kiffing him.*] Good bye,
Love.—Mr. Ledger, your fervant!—B'ye, Deareft!
[*Exit.*

HONEYCOMBE.

Ha! ha! you fee, Mr. Ledger! you fee what
you are to come to—but I beg pardon—I quite
forgot—have you breakfafted ?

LEDGER.

Breakfafted ! ay, four hours ago, and *done* an
hundred Tickets fince, over a difh cf coffee, at
Jonathan's.—Let me fee, [*pulling out his watch.*]
blefs my foul, it's eleven o'clock! I wifh Mifs
would come.—It's Transfer-Day.—I muft be at
the Bank, before twelve, without fail.

HONEYCOMBE.

Oh, here fhe comes.—[*Enter* POLLY.]—Come,
Child! where have you been all this Time?——
Well, Sir, I'll leave you together.——Polly, you'll
——ha! ha! ha!——Your fervant, Mr. Ledger,
your fervant !   [*Exit.*

[POLLY *and* LEDGER *remain,—they ftand at a great
diftance from each other.*]

POLLY. [*Afide.*]

What a monfter of a man !——What will the'
frightful creature fay to me ?——I am now, for
all the world, juft in the fituation of poor Clariffa,
——and the wretch is ten times uglier than Soames
himfelf.

LEDGER.

Well, Mifs !

C 2   POLLY.

POLLY. [*Aside.*]

' He ſpeaks! what ſhall I ſay to him?—Suppoſe
I have a little ſport with him.—I will.——I'll in-
dulge myſelf with a few airs of diſtant flirtation at
firſt, and then treat him like a dog. I'll uſe him
worſe than Nancy Howe ever did Mr. Hickman.
——Pray, Sir, [*to Ledger.*] Did you ever read the
Hiſtory of Emilia?

LEDGER.

Not I, Miſs, not I.—I have no time to think of
ſuch things, not I.—I hardly ever read any thing,
except the Daily Advertiſer, or the liſt at Lloyd's
—nor write neither, except its my name now and
then.—I keep a dozen clerks for nothing in the
world elſe but to write.

POLLY.

A dozen clerks!—Prodigious!

LEDGER.

Ay, a dozen clerks. Buſineſs muſt be done,
Miſs!—We have large returns, and the ballance
muſt be kept on the right ſide, you know,——In
regard to laſt year now——Our returns from the
firſt of January to the laſt of December, fifty-nine,
were to the amount of ſixty thouſand pounds,
ſterling. We clear upon an average, at the rate
of twelve *per cent.* Caſt up the twelves in ſixty
thouſand, and you may make a pretty good gueſs
at our net profits.

POLLY.

Net Profits!

LEDGER.

Ay, Miſs, net profits.—Simeon and Ledger are
names as well known, as any in the Alley, and
good

good for as much at the bottom of a piece of paper.———But no matter for that———you muſt know
that I have an account to ſettle with you, Miſs.——
You're on the debtor ſide in my books, I can tell
you, Miſs.

POLLY.

I in your debt, Mr. Ledger!

LEDGER.

Over head and ears in my debt, Miſs!

POLLY.

I hate to be in debt of all things———pray let
me diſcharge you at once———for I can't endure to
be dunn'd.

LEDGER.

Not ſo faſt, Miſs! not ſo faſt. Right reckoning makes long friends——Suppoſe now we ſhould
compound this matter, and ſtrike a ballance in favour of both parties.

POLLY.

How d'ye mean? Mr. Ledger!

LEDGER.

Why then in plain Engliſh, Miſs, I love you
———I'll marry you——My uncle Simeon and Mr.
Honeycombe have ſettled the matter between
them———I am fond of the match———and hope
you are the ſame———There's the Sum Total.

POLLY.

Is it poſſible that I can have any charms for Mr.
Ledger?

LEDGER

LEDGER.

Charms! Mifs; you are all over charms.——I like you—I like your perfon, your family, your fortune——I like you altogether——the Omniums ——Eh, Mifs!——I like the Omniums——and don't care how large a premium I give for them.

POLLY.

Lord, Sir!

LEDGER.

Come, Mifs, let's both fet our hands to it, and fign and feal the agreement, without lofs of time, or hindrance of bufinefs.

POLLY.

Not-fo faft, Sir, not fo faft.——Right Reckoning makes long friends, you know' — Mr. Ledger!

LEDGER.

Mifs!

POLLY.

After fo explicit and polite a declaration on your part, you will expect, no doubt, fome fuitable re- turns on mine.

LEDGER.

To be fure, Mifs, to be fure—ay, ay, let's ex- amine the *per contra*.

POLLY.

What you have faid, Mr. Ledger, has, I take it for granted, been very fincere.

LEDGER.

Very fincere, upon my credit, Mifs!

POLLY.

POLLY.

For my part then, I muſt declare, however un-
willingly———

LEDGER.

Out with it, Miſs!

POLLY.

That the paſſion I entertain for you is equally
ſtrong———

LEDGER.

Oh brave!

POLLY.

And that I do, with equal, or more ſincerity—

LEDGER.

Thank you, Miſs ; thank you!

POLLY.

Hate and deteſt———

LEDGER.

How! how!

POLLY.

Loath and abhor you———

LEDGER.

What! what!

POLLY.

Your ſight is ſhocking to me, your converſation
odious, and your paſſion contemptible———

LEDGER.

Mighty well, Miſs ; mighty well!

POLLY.

POLLY.

You are a vile book of arithmetick, a table of pounds, fhillings, and pence—You are uglier than a figure of eight, and more tirefome than the multiplication-table.——There's the Sum Total.

LEDGER.

Flefh and blood——

POLLY.

Don't talk to me—Get along—Or, if you don't leave the room, I will.

LEDGER.

Very fine, very fine, Mifs!——Mr. Honeycombe fhall know this. He'll bring you below Par again, I warrant you. [Exit.

POLLY alone.

Ha! ha! ha!——There he goes!——Ha! ha! ha!—I have out-topped them all—Mifs Howe, Narciffa, Clarinda, Polly Barnes, Sophy Willis, and all of them. None of them ever treated an odious fellow with half fo much fpirit.——This would make an excellent chapter in a new Novel.——But here comes Papa—In a violent paffion, no doubt.——No matter.——It will only furnifh materials for the next chapter.

Enter HONEYCOMBE.

HONEYCOMBE.

What is the meaning, miftrefs Polly, of this extraordinary behaviour? How dare you treat Mr. Ledger fo ill, and behave fo undutifully to your Papa and Mama?—You are a fpoilt child—Your Mama and I have been too fond of you——

10

But

But have a care, young madam! mend your con-
duct, or you may be sure, we'll make you repent
on't.

POLLY.

Lord, Papa, how can you be so angry with
me?——I am as dutiful as any girl in the world.
——But there's always an uproar in the family a-
bout marrying the daughter, and now poor I must
suffer in my turn.

HONEYCOMBE.

Hark ye, Mifs!——Why did not you receive
Mr. Ledger as your lover?

POLLY.

Lover!—Oh, dear Papa, he has no more of a
lover about him!——He never so much as caft
one languifhing look towards me, never once preft
my hand, or ftruck his breaft, or threw himfelf
at my feet, or——Lord, I read fuch a delightful
declaration of love in the new Novel this morning!-firft, Papa, fir George Trueman——

HONEYCOMBE.

Devil take fir George Trueman!——thefe curfed
Novels have turned the girl's head——Hark ye,
hufly! I could almoft find in my heart to—I fay,
hufly, isn't Mr. Ledger a hufband of your Papa
and Mama's providing? and ar'n't they the pro-
pereft perfons to difpofe of you?

POLLY.

Difpofe of me!—See there now!—Why you
have no notion of thefe things, Papa!——Your
head's fo full of trade and commerce, that you
would difpofe of your daughter like a piece of

D   merchandife

merchandife—But my heart is my own property, and at nobody's difpofal, but my own.——Sure you would not confign me, like a bale of filk, to Ledger and Co.—Eh! Papa!

HONEYCOMBE.

Her impudence amazes me.—Hark ye, huffy, you're an undutiful flut——

POLLY.

Not at all undutiful, Papa!——But I hate Mr. Ledger.——I can't endure the fight of him——

HONEYCOMBE.

This is beyond all patience.——Hark ye, huffy, I'll——

POLLY.

Nay more; to tell you the whole truth, my heart is devoted to another. I have an infuperable paffion for him; and nothing fhall fhake my affection for my dear Mr. Scribble.

HONEYCOMBE.

Mr. Scribble!—Who's Mr. Scribble?——Hark ye, huffy, I'll turn you out of doors.—I'll have you confin'd to your chamber—Get out of my fight——I'll have you lock'd up this inftant.

POLLY.

Lock'd up! I thought fo. Whenever a poor girl refufes to marry any horrid creature, her parents provide for her, then fhe's to be lock'd up immediately.——Poor Clariffa! poor Sophy Weftern! I am now going to be treated juft as you have been before me.

HONEY.

HONEYCOMBE.

Thofe abominable books!——Hark ye, huffy! you fhall have no Novel to amufe you—Get along, I fay—No pen and ink to fcrawl letters—Why don't you go?——Nor no trufty companion.—Get along——I'll have you lock'd up this inftant, and the key of your chamber fhall be in your Mama's cuftody.

POLLY.

Indeed, Papa, you need not give my Mama fo much trouble.——I have——

HONEYCOMBE.

Get along, I fay.

POLLY.

I have read of fuch things as ladders of ropes——

HONEYCOMBE.

Out of my fight!

POLLY.

Or of efcaping out of the window, by tying the fheets together——

HONEYCOMBE.

Hark ye, huffy——

POLLY.

Or of throwing one's-felf into the ftreet upon a feather-bed——

HONEYCOMBE.

I'll turn you out of doors——

POLLY.

Or of being catch'd in a gentleman's arms——

HONEYCOMBE.

Zouns, I'll——

POLLY.

Or of——

HONEYCOMBE.

Will you be gone? [*Exeunt, both talking.*

D 2 SCENE

Scene changes to POLLY's *apartment.*

Enter SCRIBBLE; *difguis'd in a livery.*

So!—In this difguife miftrefs Nurfe has brought me hither fafe and undifcover'd.——Now for Mifs Polly! here's her letter.: a true picture of her non-fenfical felf!——" To my deareft Mr. Scribble." [*Reading the direction.*] And the feal Two Doves Billing, with this motto:

" We two,
" When we wooe,
" Bill and cooe."

——Pretty!—And a plain proof I fhan't have much trouble with her.——I'll make fhort work on't——I'll carry her off to-day, if pofiible.——Clap up a marriage at once, and then down upon our marrow-bones, and afk pardon and bleffing of Papa and Mama. [*Noife without.*] Here fhe comes.

HONEYCOMBE, *without.*

Get along, I fay,——Up to your own cham-ber, huffy!

POLLY, *without.*

Well, Papa, I am——

SCRIBBLE.

O the devil!——Her father coming up with her!——What fhall I do? [*Running about.*] Where fhall I hide myfelf?—I fhall certainly be difco-vered.——I'll get up the chimney.——Zouns! they

they are juft here——Ten to one the old-cuff may
not ftay with her———I'll 'pop into this clofet.

[Exit.

Enter HONEYCOMBE and POLLY.

HONEYCOMBE.

Here, miftrefs Malapert, ftay here, if you
pleafe, and chew the cud of difobedience and mif-
chief in private.

POLLY.

Very well, Papa!

HONEYCOMBE.

Very well!——What! you are fulky now! Hark
ye, huffy, you are a faucy minx, and 'tis not very
well.———I have a good mind to keep you upon
bread and water this month. I'll—I'll—But I'll
fay no more——I'll lock you up, and carry the
key to your Mama——She'll take care of you.—
You will have Mr. Scribble.—Let's fee how he
can get to you now. [Shewing the key.]

[Exit, locking the door.

POLLY, alone.

And fo I will have Mr. Scribble too, do what
you can, Old Squaretoes!———I am provided with
pen, ink, and paper, in fpite of their teeth.———
I remember that Clariffa had cunning drawers made
on purpofe to fecure thofe things, in cafe of an
accident———I am very glad I have had caution
enough to provide myfelf with the fame imple-
ments of intrigue, tho' with a little more ingenu-
ity.———Indeed now they make ftandifhes, and
tea-chefts, and dreffing boxes, in all forts of fhapes
and figures———But mine are of my own inven-
tion.

tion.————Here I've got an excellent ink-horn in
my pin-cuſhion—And a caſe of pens, and ſome
paper, in my fan. [*Produces them.*] I will write to
Mr. Scribble immediately. I ſhall certainly ſee
him eaves-dropping about our door the firſt opportunity, and then I'll toſs it to him out of the window. [*Sits down to write:*

S C R I B B L E, *putting his head out of the door of the
cloſet.*

A clear coaſt, I find————The old Codger's
gone, and has lock'd me up with his daughter—
So much the better!—Pretty Soul! what is ſhe
about? Writing?—A letter to me, I'll bet ten to
one.————I'll go and anſwer it in *propriâ perſonâ.*

[*Comes forward, and ſtands behind* Polly,
looking over her writing.

P O L L Y, *writing.*
" Me—in—your—Arms."————Let me ſee——
What have I written? [*Reading.*] " My deareſt
" dear, Mr. Scribble.

S C R I B B L E.
I thought ſo!

P O L L Y, *reading.*
" I am now writing in the moſt cruel confine-
" ment. Fly then, oh fly to me on the wings of
" love, releaſe me from this horrid gaol, and im-
" priſon me in your arms."

S C R I B B L E.
That I will with all my heart. [*Embracing her,*

P O L L Y.
Oh! [*Screaming.*]

S C R I B B L E.

SCRIBBLE.

O the devil!—why do you fcream fo.?—I fhall
be difcovered in fpite of fortune. [*running about.*]

POLLY.

Blefs me! is it you? Hufh! [*running to the door.*]
here's my father coming up ftairs, I proteft.

SCRIBBLE.

What the duce fhall I do?————I'll run into
the clofet again.

POLLY.

O no! he'll fearch the clofet————Jump out
of the window!

SCRIBBLE.

I beg to be excus'd.

POLLY.

Lord! here's no time to—he's here—get under
the table————[Scribble *hides.*]—Lie ftill—What
fhall I fay? [*fits down by the table.*]

Enter HONEYCOMBE.

HONEYCOMBE.

How now? huffy!—What's all this noife?

POLLY.

Sir! [*affecting furprize.*]

HONEYCOMBE.

What made you fcream fo violently?

POLLY.

Scream! Papa?

HONEYCOMBE.

Scream? Papa!—Ay, fcream, huffy!—What
made you fcream? I fay.

POLLY.

POLLY.

"Lord, Papa, I have never opened my lips, but have been in a philosophical reverie ever since you left me.

HONEYCOMBE.

I am sure I thought I heard———But, how now, huffy! what's here?—pens—ink—and paper!——Hark ye, huffy!—How came you by thefe?—So! fo! fine contrivances! *[Examining them]*—And a letter begun too——"cruel con- " finement——wings of love——your arms." [*reading.*] Ah, you forward flut!——But I am glad I have difcovered this——I'll feize thefe moveables.——So! fo! now write, if you can.—Nobody fhall come near you——Send to him, if you can.——Now fee how Mr. Scribble will get at you.——Now I have you fafe, miftrefs!—and now—ha! ha!—now you may make love to the table.——Hey-day! what's here? a man! [*Seeing* Scribble.] There was a noife then. Have I caught you? madam!——Come, Sir, come out of your hole! [Scribble *comes from under the table.*] A footman!—Who the devil are you? Sir!—Where did you come from?—What d'ye want?——How came you here? eh, firrah!

SCRIBBLE.

Sir—I—I—What the duce fhall I fay to him?

HONEYCOMBE.

Speak, rafcal!

SCRIBBLE.

Sir—I—I—I came about a little bufinefs to Mifs Honeycombe.

HONEYCOMBE.

Bufinefs!—Ay, you look like a man of bufinefs indeed——What! you was to carry this fcrawl of a love-letter, I suppofe. Eh, firrah!

SCRIBBLE.

SCRIBBLE.

A lucky miftake! I'll humour it.   [*Afide.*

HONEYCOMBE.

What's that you mutter?——Whofe livery is this? who do you belong to? fellow!

SCRIBBLE.

My mafter.

HONEYCOMBE.

And who is your mafter, Sir?

SCRIBBLE.

A gentleman.

POLLY.

Papa don't fufpect who he is. I muft fpeak for him. [*Afide.*]——This honeft young man belongs to the gentleman I told you I was devoted to—Mr. Scribble, Papa!

HONEYCOMBE.

To Mr. Scribble, does he? Very fine!

SCRIBBLE.

Yes, Sir! to Mr. Scribble——a perfon of fortune and character——A man of fafhion, Sir!—Mifs Polly need not blufh to own her paffion for him—I don't know a finer gentleman about town than Mr. Scribble.

POLLY.

Lord, how well he behaves!—We fhall certainly bam the old gentleman.   [*Afide.*

HONEYCOMBE.

Hark ye, firrah!—Get out of my houfe this inftant.——I've a good mind to have you toffed in a blanket——or dragged thro' a horfe-pond——or tied neck and heels, and——I've a good mind to carry you before the Sitting Alderman, you dog you?

E   SCRIBBLE.

SCRIBBLE.

I won't give you that trouble, Sir!——Mifs Honeycombe, I kifs your hands.——You have no further commands to my mafter, at prefent? Ma'am!——Your compliments, I fuppofe.

POLLY.

Compliments!——My beft love to my dear Mr. Scribble.

SCRIBBLE.

Pretty foul!

HONEYCOMBE.

This is beyond all patience.---Out of my houfe, firrah!——Where are all my fellows?——I'll have you thrown out of the window.——You fhall be trundled down ftairs headlong—You fhall——

SCRIBBLE.

Patience, old gentleman! I fhall go out of the houfe the fame way I came into it, I promife you!——And let me tell you, Sir, by way of a kind word at parting, that fcold Mifs Polly ever fo much, watch her ever fo narrowly, or confine her ever fo clofely, Mr. Scribble will have her, whether you will or no, you old cuff, you! [*Exit.*

HONEYCOMBE.

An impudent dog!—I'll have his livery ftript over his ears for his infolence.—As for you, my young miftrefs, I'll bring down your high fpirit, I warrant you.——There, ma'am, fit there if you pleafe! [*forcing her into a chair.*] We'll fend you the Whole Duty of Man, or the Practice of Piety to read,—or a chair, a fcreen, or a carpet to work with your needle.—We'll find you employment.—Some other books than Novels, and fome better company than Mr. Scribble's footman.——Have
done

done with your nonfenfe—and learn to make a pudding, you impudent, idle young baggage!

[Exit.

POLLY, alone.

An old fool! [mocking him.] Well! this is a curious adventure truly!—If I could but make my efcape now, after all, it would be admirable. —I am fure Mr. Scribble would not go far from the houfe.——Let me fee—how can I manage it? —Suppofe I force the lock—or take off the fcrews of it—or get the door off the hinges.——I'll try. [Going, ftops.] Or hold! I have a brighter thought than any of them——I'll fet fire to the houfe—— and fo be carried off, like ftolen goods, in the con- fufion.——A moft excellent contrivance!—I muft put it in práctice. [Noife without.] O dear, here's fomebody coming.——[After unlocking the door, Enter Nurfe.] Oh, Nurfe, is it you? I am heartily glad to fee you. I thought it had been Papa, or Mama.

NURSE.

Ah, Chicken, I have taken care of your Ma- ma.——Mr. Honeycombe brought her the key in a parlous fury, with orders to let nobody go near you, except himfelf. But Madam—I can't chufe but laugh—Madam had taken a glafs extraordina- ry of her cordial, and I have left her faft afleep in her own chamber.

POLLY.

The luckieft thing in the world!——Now, my dear Nurfee, you may let your poor bird out of her cage.——Away, away this inftant!

NURSE.

Softly, Chicken, foftly!—you ruined all with Mr. Scribble, juft now, by making a noife, you know.

E 2   POLLY.

POLLY.

Lord, Nurfee, I had no power of reflection—I was quite frightened——I was as much furprifed as Sophy Weftern when fhe faw Tom Jones in the looking-glafs.

NURSE.

Hufh! you fhall fteal off immediately. Your Papa is very bufy with Mr. Ledger.——Mr. Scribble is waiting with a hackney chair but in the next ftreet—you may flip flily into it, and be convey'd to his lodging in a trice, Chicken!

POLLY.

And he ftrut before the chair all the way in his livery, and cry—" By your leave, Sir!—By your " leave, Ma'am!"—Eh!—Admirable!——Come, Nurfee, I long to be in his hands.

NURSE.

Stay! let me go before, to fee that there is nobody in the way. Come gently down ftairs.——I'll fet open the door, and then you may get to him as faft as you can.—Ah, you're a wanton baggage!

POLLY.

Very well! come along then!——" By your " leave, Sir!—By your leave, Ma'am!" Oh rare!——This is the fineft adventure I ever had in my life.   [Exit, following the Nurfe.

Scene changes to Mrs. HONEYCOMBE's *Apartment.*

Mrs. HONEYCOMBE *alone,—feveral phials on the table, with labels.*

I am not at all well to-day.—[yawns, as if juft waking.]—Such a quantity of tea in a morning,

makes

makes one quite Nervous—and Mr. Honeycombe does not chuse it qualified.——I have such a dizziness in my head, it absolutely turns round with me.—I don't think neither that the Hysterick Water is warm enough for my stomach.——I must speak to Mr. Julep to order me something rather more comfortable.

Enter NURSE.

NURSE.

Did you call, Ma'am?.

Mrs. HONEYCOMBE.

Oh Nurse, is it you?—No, I did not call——Where's Mr. Honeycombe?

NURSE.

Below stairs in the parlour, Madam——I did not think she'd have wak'd so soon—If she should miss the key now, before I've an opportunity to lay it down again! [*Aside.*].

Mrs. HONEYCOMBE.

What d'ye say, Nurse?

NURSE.

Say? Ma'am!——Say!——I say, I hope you're a little better, Ma'am!

Mrs. HONEYCOMBE.

Oh Nurse, I am perfectly giddy with my Nerves, and so low-spirited.

NURSE.

Poor gentlewoman! suppose I give you a sup out of the case of Italian Cordials, Ma'am! that was sent as a present from Mr. What-d'ye-call-him, in Crutched-Fryars—The Italian Merchant with the long name.

Mrs.

Mrs. HONEYCOMBE.

Filthy poifon! don't mention it!—Faugh! I hate the very names of them.—You know, Nurfe, I never touch any Cordials, but what come from the Apothecary's——What o'clock is it?——Isn't it time to take my Draught?

NURSE.

By my troth, I believe it is—Let me fee, I believe this is it——[*Takes up a phial, and flips the key upon the table.*] " The Stomachick Draught to " be taken an hour before dinner. For Mrs. Ho- " neycombe." [*reading the label.*]—Ay, this is it ——By my troth, I am glad I've got rid of the key again. [*Afide.*]

Mrs. HONEYCOMBE.

Come then!—Pour it into a tea cup, and give it me.—I'm afraid I can't take it. It goes fadly againft me.

While fhe is drinking, HONEYCOMBE *without.*

Run, John, run!—After them immediately!— Harry, do you run too——Stick clofe to Mr. Ledger——Don't return without them for your life!

NURSE.

Good lack! good lack! they're difcovered as fure as the day. [*Afide.*]

Mrs. HONEYCOMBE.

Lord, Nurfe, what's the matter?

NURSE.

I don't know, by my troth.

Enter

Enter HONEYCOMBE.

Mrs. HONEYCOMBE.

O, my Sweeting, I am glad you are come.—I was so frighted about you. [*Rises, and seems disordered.*]

HONEYCOMBE.

Zouns, my Dear————

Mrs. HONEYCOMBE.

O don't swear, my Dearest!

HONEYCOMBE.

Zouns, it's enough to make a parson swear——You have let Polly escape——She's run away with a fellow.

Mrs. HONEYCOMBE.

You perfectly astonish me, my Dear!——I can't possibly conceive——My poor head aches too to such a degree——Where's the key of her chamber? [*Seems disordered.*]

NURSE.

Here, Madam, here it is.

HONEYCOMBE.

Zouns, I tell you——

Mrs. HONEYCOMBE.

Why here's the key, my Sweeting!——It's absolutely impossible—it has lain here ever since you brought it me—not a soul has touched it—have they, Nurse? [*disordered.*]

NURSE.

NURSE.

Not a creature, I'll take my Bible oath on't.

HONEYCOMBE.

I tell you, she's gone.——I'm sure on't——Mr. Ledger saw a strange footman put her into a chair, at the corner of the street—and He and John, and a whole Posse, are gone in persuit of them.

Mrs. HONEYCOMBE.

This is the most extraordinary circumstance—— It's quite beyond my comprehension——But my Sweeting must not be angry with his own dear wife—it was not her fault. [*fondling.*]

HONEYCOMBE.

Nay, my Love, don't trifle now!——

Mrs. HONEYCOMBE.

I must——I will——

HONEYCOMBE.

Zouns, my Dear, be quiet!—I shall have my girl ruined for ever.

LEDGER, *without.*

This way—this way—bring them along!

HONEYCOMBE.

Hark! they're coming—Mr. Ledger has over-taken them——they're here.

LEDGER, *without.*

Here!—Mr. Honeycombé is in this room—— Come along!

Enter

Enter LEDGER, POLLY, *and* SCRIBBLE,
with Servants.

L E D G E R.

Here they are, Mr. Honeycombe!——We've
brought them back again.——Here they are,
Madam.

H O N E Y C O M B E.

Hark ye, Huffy! I have a good mind to turn
you out of doors again immediately.——You are
a difgrace to your family.—You're a fhame to——

Mrs. H O N E Y C O M B E.

Stay, my dear, don't you put yourfelf into fuch
a paffion!——Polly, obferve what I fay to you—
Let me know the whole circumftances of this affair——I don't at all underftand——Tell me,
I fay——[*Diforder'd.*]

H O N E Y C O M B E.

Zouns! I have no patience.—Hark ye, huffy!
——Where was you going?——Tell me for certain who this fellow belongs to?——Where does
he live?——Who is he?

P O L L Y.

That gentleman, Papa, that gentleman is no
other than Mr. Scribble.

H O N E Y C O M B E.

This! is this Mr. Scribble?

S C R I B B L E.

The very man, fir, at your fervice——An hum-
ble admirer of Mifs Honeycombe's.

F POLLY.

POLLY.

Yes, Papa, that's Mr. Scribble.———The fo-
vereign of my heart———The fole object of my af-
fections.

Mrs. HONEYCOMBE.

What can be the meaning of all this?

HONEYCOMBE.

Why, you beggarly flut! this is even worfe
than I expected.———What, would you run away
from your family with a fellow in livery? a footman?

POLLY.

A footman! ha! ha! ha! very good; and, fo,
Papa, you really believe he is a footman. A footman!

SCRIBBLE.

A footman, eh, my dear!———An errand boy!
———A fcoundrel fellow in livery———Yes, I am
very like a footman, to be fure! [*Laughing with*
Polly.]

POLLY,

Why, Papa, don't you know that every gentleman difguifes himfelf in the courfe of an amour?
———Don't you remember that Bob Lovelace dif-
guifed himfelf like an old man? and Tom Ramble like an old woman?———No adventure can
be carried on without it.

HONEYCOMBE.

She's certainly mad—ftark mad.———Hark ye,
fir! who are you?———I'll have you fent to the
Compter—You fhall give an account of yourfelf
before my Lord Mayor.

SCRIBBLE.

S C R I B B L E.

What care I for my Lord-Mayor?

H O N E Y C O M B E.

There!—There's a fellow for you!—Don't care
for my Lord-Mayor!

S C R I B B L E.

No—nor the whole court of Aldermen.—Hark
ye, old Greybeard, I am a gentleman——A gentleman as well known, as any in the city.

Mrs. H O N E Y C O M B E.

Upon my word, I believe so.—He seems a very
proper gentleman-like—sort of a—kind of a—per-
son.

L E D G E R.

As well known as any in the city!——I don't
believe it—He's no good man—I am sure he's not
known upon Change.

S C R I B B L E.

Damme, sir; what d'ye mean?

L E D G E R.

Oho! Mr. Gentleman, is it you?——I thought,
I knew your voice—Ay, and your face too.——
Pray, sir, don't you live with Mr. Traverse, the
attorney, of Gracechurch-Street?——Did not you
come to me last week about a policy of insurance?

S C R I B B L E.

O the Devil! [*aside.*] I come to you? sir!——
I never saw your face before. [*to* Ledger.]

N U R S E.

Good lack! he'll certainly be discovered. [*aside.*

H O N E Y C O M B E.

An attorney's clerk!——Hark ye, friend——

F 3   S C R I B B L E.

SCRIBBLE.

'Egad, I'd beſt ſneak off before it's worſe.
[*going.*

HONEYCOMBE.

Hark ye, woman! [*to* Nurſe.]——I begin to
ſuſpect—Have not I heard you ſpeak of a kinſ-
man, clerk to Mr. Traverſe?——Stop him!

SCRIBBLE.

Hands off, Gentlemen!——Well then—I do go
through a little buſineſs for Mr. Traverſe—What
then? What have you to ſay to me now? ſir!

POLLY.

Do pray, Mama, take Mr. Scribble's part, pray do!

NURSE.

Do, ma'am, ſpeak a good word
for him.

Mrs. HONEYCOMBE.

I underſtand nothing at all of the
matter.

*Apart, while
they are
ſtopping
Scribble.*

HONEYCOMBE.

Hark ye, Woman!——He's your nephew—
I'm ſure on't——I'll turn you out of doors immediately.——You ſhall be——

NURSE.

I beg upon my knees that your honour would
forgive me——I meant no harm, Heaven above
knows——   [*Kneeling.*

HONEYCOMBE.

No harm! what, to marry my daughter to——
I'll have you ſent to Newgate——And you, [*to*
Polly.] you ſorry baggage; d'ye ſee what you was
about?——You was running away with a beggar
—With your Nurſe's nephew, huſſy!

POLLY.

P O L L Y,

Lord, Papa, what fignifies whofe nephew he is? He may be ne'er the worfe for that.—Who knows but he may be a Foundling, and a gentleman's fon, as well as Tom Jones?—My mind is refolv-ed,——And nothing fhall ever alter it.

S C R I B B L E.

Bravo, Mifs Polly!——A fine generous fpirit, faith!

H O N E Y C O M B E.

You're an impudent flut—You're undone.——

Mrs. H O N E Y C O M B E.

Nay, but, look ye, Polly!—mind me, child! ——You know that I——.

P O L L Y.

As for my poor Mama here, you fee, fir, fhe is a little in the nervous way, this morning—— When fhe comes to herfelf, and Mr. Julep's draughts have taken a proper effect, fhe'll be convinced I am in the right.

H O N E Y C O M B E.

Hold your impertinence!—Hark ye, Polly--—

P O L L Y.

And you, my angelick Mr. Scribble!

S C R I B B L E.

Ma chere Adorable!

P O L L Y.

You may depend on my conftancy and affection. I never read of any Lady's giving up her lover, to fubmit to the abfurd election of her parents—— I'll have you, let what will be the confequence. ——I'll have you, though we go through as many diftreffes as Booth and Amelia.

H O N E Y.

HONEYCOMBE.

Peace, huffy!

POLLY.

As for you, you odious Wretch, [*to* Ledger.] how could they ever imagine that I should dream of such a creature? A great He-monster! I would as soon be married to the Staffordshire Giant——I hate you. You are as deceitful as Blifil, as rude as the Harlowes, and as ugly as Doctor Slop.

[*Exit.*

LEDGER.

Mighty well, Miſs, mighty well!

SCRIBBLE.

Prodigious humour! high fun, faith!

HONEYCOMBE.

She's downright raving—Mad as a March hare ——I'll put her into Bedlam——I'll send her into the country——I'll have her shut up in a nunnery ——I'll——

Mrs. HONEYCOMBE.

Come, my Sweeting, don't make your dear self so uneaſy—Don't——

HONEYCOMBE.

As for you, fir! [*to* Scribble.]—Hark ye, Stripling——

SCRIBBLE.

Nay, nay, Old Gentleman, no bouncing!—— You're miſtaſten in your man, fir! I know what I'm about.

HONEYCOMBE.

Zouns, fir, and I know——

SCRIBBLE,

SCRIBBLE.

Yes, fir, and I know that I've done nothing contrary to the twenty-fixth of the King—Above a month ago, fir, I took lodgings in Mifs Polly's name and mine, in the parifh of St. George's in the Fields————The bans have been afked three times, and I could have married Mifs Polly to-day ————So much for that,————And fo, fir, your fervant.————If you offer to detain me, I fhall bring my action on the cafe for falfe imprifonment, fue out a bill of Middlefex, and upon a *Non eft inventus*, if you abfcond, a *Latitat*, then an *Alias*, a *Pluries*, a *Non omittas*, and fo on————Or perhaps I may indict you at the feffions, bring the affair by *Certiorari* into *Bancum regis*, *et cætera*, *et cætera*, *et cætera*————And now————Stop me at your peril. [*Exit.*

HONEYCOMBE.

I am ftunn'd with his jargon, and confounded at his impudence.————Hark you, woman, [*to the* Nurfe.]—I'll have you committed to Newgate —I'll————

NURSE.

Mighty well, your honour!————Fine treatment for an old fervant indeed!————I, to be huff'd and ding'd about at this rate;————But 'tis an old faying and a true one—Give a dog an ill name, and hang him!—Live and learn, as they fay———— We grow older and older every day.————Service is no inheritance in thefe ages————There are more places than parifh-churches————So you may do as you pleafe, your honour!————But I fhall look up my things! give up a month's wages, for want of a month's warning, and go my ways out of your houfe immediately. [*Exit.*

HONEY-

HONEYCOMBE.

Why, you old beldam, I'll have you carted——
You ſhall be burnt for a witch——But I'll put
an end to this matter at once——Mr. Ledger,
you ſhall marry my daughter to-morrow morning.

LEDGER.

Not I, indeed my friend! I give up my intereſt
in her.——She'd make a terrible wife for a ſober
citizen.——Who can anſwer for her behaviour?
——I would not underwrite her for ninety *per
cent.* [*Exit.*

HONEYCOMBE.

See there! ſee there!—My girl is undone.—Her
character is ruined with all the world——Theſe
damn'd Story Books!—What ſhall we do, Mrs.
Honeycombe? what ſhall we do?

Mrs. HONEYCOMBE.

·Look ye, my Dear, you've been wrong in every
particular——

HONEYCOMBE.

Wrong!——I! Wrong!——

Mrs. HONEYCOMBE.

Quite wrong, my Dear!——I wou'd not expoſe
you before company—My Tenderneſs, you know,
is ſo great——But leave the whole affair to me-—
You are too violent——Go, my dear, go and
compoſe yourſelf, and I'll ſet all matters to rights
——[*Going, turns back.*] Don't you do any thing
of your own head now—Truſt it all to me, my
Dear!—And I'll ſettle it in ſuch a manner, that
you,—and I—and all the world—ſhall be aſtoniſh-
ed and delighted with it. [*Exit muttering.*

HONEYCOMBE *alone.*

Zouns, I ſhall run mad with vexation—Was
ever man ſo heartily provoked?—You ſee now,
Gentlemen, [*coming forward to the audience.*] what

a

a fituation I am in!—Inftead of happinefs and jol-
lity—My friends and family about me,—A wed-
ding and a dance,—And every thing as it fhould
be,—Here am I, left by myfelf,—Deferted by my
intended fon-in-law—Bully'd by an attorney's clerk
—Affronted by my own fervant—My Daughter
mad—My Wife in the Vapours—And all's in confufion.——This comes of Cordials and Novels.—
Zouns, your Stomachicks are the Devil—And a
man might as well turn his Daughter loofe in Co-
vent-garden, as truft the cultivation of her mind
to

A CIRCULATING LIBRARY.

G   E P I.

EPILOGUE.

Written by Mr. GARRICK,

Spoken by Miss POPE.

Enter, as POLLY, *laughing*—Ha! ha! ha!

*M*Y *poor Papa's in woeful agitation—*
While I, the Cause, feel here, [ſtriking her
boſom.] *no palpitation.—*
We Girls of Reading, and ſuperior notions,
Who from the fountain-head drink love's ſweet potions,
Pity our parents, when ſuch paſſion blinds 'em,
One hears the good folks rave—One never minds 'em.
Till theſe dear books infuſ'd their ſoft ingredients,
Aſham'd and fearful, I was all Obedience.
Then my good Father did not ſtorm in vain,
I bluſh'd and cry'd—I'll ne'er do ſo again:
But now no bugbears can my ſpirit tame,
I've conquer'd Fear—And almoſt conquer'd Shame;
So much theſe Dear Inſtructors change and win us,
Without their light we ne'er ſhould know what's in us.
Here we at once ſupply our childiſh wants—
Novels are Hotbeds for your forward plants.
Not only Sentiments refine the Soul,
But hence we learn to be the Smart and Drole;
Each aukward circumſtance for laughter ſerves,
From Nurſe's nonſenſe to my Mother's Nerves:

Though

EPILOGUE

Though Parents tell us, that our genius lies
In mending linen and in making pies,
I set such formal precepts at defiance
That preach up prudence, neatness, and compliance;
Leap these old bounds, and boldly set the pattern,
To be a Wit, Philosopher, and Slattern——

O! did all Maids and Wives my spirit feel,
We'd make this topsy-turvy world to reel:
Let us to arms!——Our Fathers, Husbands, dare!
Novels will teach us all the Art of War:
Our Tongues will serve for Trumpet and for Drum;
I'll be your Leader——General Honeycombe!

Too long has human nature gone astray,
Daughters should govern, Parents should obey;
Man should submit, the moment that he weds,
And hearts of oak should yield to wiser heads:
I see you smile, bold Britons!——*But 'tis true——*
Beat You *the* French;——*But let your* Wives *beat*
* You.——*

FINIS.

Printed in the United States
109392LV00018B/153/A